LOVE FOR . . .

TEN SESSION OUTLINES
FOR CHILDREN

NICK HARDING

Kevin Mayhew

First published in 2000 by
KEVIN MAYHEW LTD
Buxhall
Stowmarket
Suffolk IP14 3BW

0 1 2 3 4 5 6 7 8 9

ISBN 1 84003 646 X
Catalogue No. 1500391

Cover design by Jonathan Stroulger
Illustrations by Simon Smith
Edited by Katherine Laidler
Typesetting by Kevin Whomes
Printed in Great Britain

Contents

About the author

Nick Harding grew up in Birmingham, found faith at a Baptist Church, spent student days in Devon, taught for a few years near Nottingham, and has been up to his eyes in children's and youth work ever since! He lives near Sherwood Forest with his wife and two energetic sons, loves the music of Elton John and Elgar, supports Aston Villa, is a member of the Mothers' Union, and travels on buses as a hobby! He works for his local cathedral, Southwell Minster, as Schools Officer where he also runs an award-winning educational project called 'Time Travelling!' He loves preaching, which he does every Sunday at churches of most denominations and traditions. Best recent moment – being really busy with a new challenge. Worst recent moment – fluffing the first line of a 'thought for the day' on BBC local radio!

Introduction

- Have you ever been stuck for material, and found that the time you put aside to plan has vanished?
- Have you ever struggled to use published material because it assumes the children have good Bible knowledge?

These are problems faced by everyone who works with children, whether in church or school. These session outlines are designed to meet your needs, with easy-to-prepare and varied material, including plenty of activity and lots for children to think about. They are aimed at children on the fringe of the church and those outside – perhaps who come to a holiday club, attend a midweek group, or go to the Christian group at school. They are intended for the 7-12 age group, but are adaptable for use with both younger and older groups. All the material here has been tried and tested over a number of years, and should provide all you need to help young people with no church experience get to grips with the nature of the Christian faith and ultimately God's love for them.

Each outline follows the same pattern, giving a number of sections which can be used. Remember that there is probably too much for one session, and you may want to miss items out or do them the following week. Other suggestions may be unsuitable for your group or facilities.

Theme

At the start of each outline is a clearly defined theme. This is to help you understand the point that the games, stories and talk suggestions are working towards.

Active game

There is at least one active game suggestion during each outline. This is provided to enable the young people to let off steam in a fun way, with a connection to the theme of the session.

Game

There is often another game which involves some of the group. Be aware that when asking for 'volunteers' you need to aim for a balance of boys and girls, able and less able, and so on.

Illustration

There are simple illustrations for a leader to act out included in some of these outlines. They introduce the theme of the session.

Quiz

Many of the outlines have a quiz suggestion to enable you to reinforce the point, or to introduce the theme. These are not meant to be too competitive, and shouldn't be taken too seriously!

Discussion

A vital skill to learn is the ability to express a point of view in a supportive environment. Discussion suggestions are provided to help you explore the theme and develop the children's skills in giving and receiving information.

Talk

It is sometimes necessary for you to be clear about what you want to say rather than have a discussion. Some outlines include talks, with the main points listed.

Craft

These outlines include a craft suggestion where suitable and relevant. Most children learn best by doing, so it's good to include as much activity as possible in your plans. The craft suggestions include a minimum of equipment and resources.

Bible input

Every outline includes a Bible reference and a suggestion as to how you may want to tell the story. Remember that the children may be unfamiliar with the Bible, and it should always be presented in a positive and lively manner.

Prayer

At the end of each outline is a prayer or a prayer suggestion. These vary from quiet and meditative to lively, aimed at children who are not used to praying and who may be embarrassed by it.

Memory chant

Each outline includes a simple chant on the theme of that day. These could be learned, remembered, repeated each session and added to as you go along, giving all the group members some basic truths to remember.

Songs

There are suggested songs given, but don't be restricted by this list. Most of them can be found in a large number of books from various publishers, including

ICC *Spring Harvest*

Scripture Union *Everybody Praise*

HarperCollins *Junior Praise*

Kevin Mayhew *Kidsource*

You may know and use much more relevant and suitable songs!

Funsheet

This is for you to photocopy and use either as part of the session or to give the children to take home and complete. It complements the session but does not have to be used at the same time. Ingredients include wordsearches, questions, puzzles, prayers, thought starters and quizzes.

You need to add...

(a) time for registration, notices, chatting, tuck shop, and whatever else is a normal part of your regular meetings.

(b) your own wisdom, energy and creativity to make these outlines work for you and your young people.

Other suggestions

- Use these outlines for a holiday club, decorating the room with 'Love 4' and using it on the publicity posters and leaflets.
- Use the chant 'Love, one, two, three! Love for you and love for me!' to a regular clapping rhythm. This helps reinforce the teaching message for the ten outlines.
- If you have limited time each week split each of the sessions into two, providing a balance of activity and quiet in each.
- Try saying 'Amen' in a different way – shouting, winding up (ameeeeeeeeen), 'I agree' or 'Hey, that's cool!'

I hope *Love for . . .* helps you do your job with children more effectively, and I hope that through it more young people will come to know the life and love of Jesus for themselves.

With special thanks to
Clare, Jared and Callum

For all children's workers who care
about those outside the church

Session 1 Love for . . . the world

Theme

God created the world for everyone, and he shows his love for us through it.

Active game

You will need an inflatable globe the size of a football. These are readily available to buy; alternatively you could draw a basic outline of the world on to a large ball.

The children should spread out in the room while you and another leader roll the globe towards them. If the globe hits a child's legs they must pick it up and speak for 30 seconds about a country or continent. Then the game continues.

Illustration

Pick up the globe. Talk about how exciting and interesting the world is. Mention the theories that say that the world was developed out of an accidental explosion of gasses, and explain that the Bible, God's book, tells us that he made it. Ask the children to think about whether the world as we know it could have been just an accident.

Bible input

To tell this version of the creation account you will need the items in italics. As each new day begins ask for a volunteer to come forward and hold the item.

In the beginning there was nothing. It wasn't light, dry or wet. There was no smell, no movement, no sky or land.

Torch. Then God decided to create light and dark, and in a word it was done. He separated the dark from the light, calling one 'night' and the other 'day'. At the end of that first day the world had begun to be made.

Cup of water. The next day God decided to separate the water from the air around it, and so he made sky. He put the sky high above and the water below it.

An apple. God decided that on the following day he would create land that was to be surrounded by the sea, and he made things grow on the land. There were plants, bushes and trees, many of which produced fruit or grain.

A cardboard star. Then God made his mind up to fill the sky with lights, stars and planets, including the sun to give light during the day and the moon for the night. This was to show that there is more to God's creation than just the world!

A real fish. The sea was soon filled with fish and other creatures that God made, and the trees became the home for birds which flew in the sky. Each one was made by God, and every one was different from another.

Animal puppet and a child. God made animals next. He made animals to walk on the land and live in holes or under sheltering trees. Some were small, others large. Some were beautiful, and others rather odd.

Then God finished the world off with people to live there. First he created a man, Adam, and then Eve to live with him and keep him company. They had a wonderful world to live in, full of new life and beauty. God loved people then, and he loves people now.

Discussion

Wrong world

Ask the children to be quiet for one minute to think about all the bad things happening in the world that are caused by humans. Check recent news items about global warming, oil spills, pollution and deforestation to get the discussion started. End by asking the following questions:

- What did God think of the world he had made?
- Do people love the world as much as God loves it?
- What can we do to love the world more?

Craft activity

World collage

Put together or cut out a circle of thick paper or card with a diameter of at least one metre. Place this in the middle of the floor, and have available paints, crayons, paper, magazines, holiday brochures and newspapers. The children should cut out pictures or draw their own. One half of the circle should show the good things about the world that God made, and the other should have some of the bad things that people have done to the world.

Quiz

What first?

Split the group into two, and have sweets ready to throw to each child who answers correctly. Award two points for each correct answer. Each question is based on the Bible narrative earlier, and begins, 'What did God make first?'

1. What did God make first – man or woman?	man
2. What did God make first – animals or birds?	birds
3. What did God make first – sky or light?	light
4. What did God make first – trees or sea?	sea
5. What did God make first – stars or night?	night

6. What did God make first – fish or man? fish
7. What did God make first – plants or sea creatures? plants
8. What did God make first – earth or darkness? darkness

Prayer

Make a list of some of the good things in the world that God made. Ask the children whether they have seen any memorable, beautiful natural scenes and add those to the list. Then mention each one in turn, each time with the response:

Thank you, God, that you love the world.

Then make a list of the bad things in the world. Again, ask the group for suggestions. Mention those in turn, with the response:

We are sorry, God, for not loving your world.

Memory chant

The first chant in this series is:

The world with everything above
is a sign of God's great love!

Songs

Who put the colours in the rainbow?
Everything comes from God
Before you made the skies and seas
My God is so big

LOVE 4

1. Love for... the World.

DAY 4: Stars

Draw Pictures...

DAY 6: Animals

..and God said..

...fill in the gaps...

MY PERFECT WORLD

What would it be like? Write here

Chant

The World
with everything
above
is a sign of
God's
great love!

Session 2 Love for . . . animals

Theme

God loves the world and everything he made in it, including animals.

Active game

For each game the children need to work in pairs.

1. *Stand up.* The children sit on the floor back to back and link arms. Then, without using their hands or going on to their knees, they must push against each other to stand up.
2. *Mirror.* The children take it in turns to do movements and actions, with the partner facing them trying to mirror everything they do.
3. *Animals.* One of the pair must pretend to be an animal, while the other one tries to guess what animal it is. Then they swap over, with the other having a go, and so on.

Game

Yes

Ask for a volunteer to come to the front. Then ask them questions about an animal of your choosing. They must answer all the questions you ask, but are out of the game if they answer with a 'Yes'. Repeat this with other volunteers as time allows.

Bible input

Read an account of Noah and the flood, whether from the Bible (Genesis 6:9-8:19) or a story book, or use your own version. Make sure you cover these points:

- God washed the world because people were making it bad.
- Noah built the ark as a response to God.
- God told Noah to take two of each animal and bird into the ark.
- The rains lasted for 40 days.
- After dry land was discovered the animals and birds were released to live on earth again.

Discussion

Try to lead the children into thinking more about the Bible story by asking the following questions:

- Why was the world going wrong?
- What do you think other people thought of Noah and his family as they built their boat miles from the sea?

- Why did God tell Noah to take two of each animal and bird into the ark?
- What happened to the people and animals that were not in the ark?
- What did the animals do when the boat doors were finally opened?
- Why did God want to save animals as well as people?

Craft

Masks

Have some sheets of thin card (A3 size is best) and elastic available, along with pens, crayons, a stapler and scissors. Ask the children to create their own masks of real or imaginary animals, cut out the shape and eye holes, and fix elastic to the back so that they can be worn. Older children may want to do pictures instead of making masks to wear.

Talk

God didn't want to wash the world with a great flood, but the people had gone wrong and he wanted to give humankind a chance to start again. God loves all that he created, including animals. He tells people to rule over animals, but doesn't say we should be unnecessarily cruel to them. Many people think that eating meat from animals is cruel, but others, like most people in the Bible, see meat and animals as another of God's gifts to us.

As the two of each animal left the ark and went away, settled down and had cubs, calves or puppies, God gave us all animals to enjoy. We may have a pet that makes us happy, or remember seeing deer in the wild and thinking how beautiful they are. God loves his creation, including all of us, and including animals.

Activity game

Animal A-Z

Stand the group in a circle. Start off by naming an animal beginning with A, while the person to your left must think of an animal beginning with B, and so on. If the child can't think of one move on to the next person. You could add a slight competitive edge by getting those who are successful in naming an animal to sit down once they have done so.

Prayer

Ask the children to be quiet and think about animals, either those they have seen or those they have as pets. Invite them to say a prayer in their minds, thanking God that he loves everything he made, including animals.

Memory chant

Here is the one for this session:

Whether they've got legs or wings,
God's love is for all living things!

Songs

Down in the jungle
A wiggly worm
Everything comes from God
Rise and shine

LOVE 4

2. Love for ... Animals.

Chant

Whether they've got legs or wings,
God's love is for all living things!

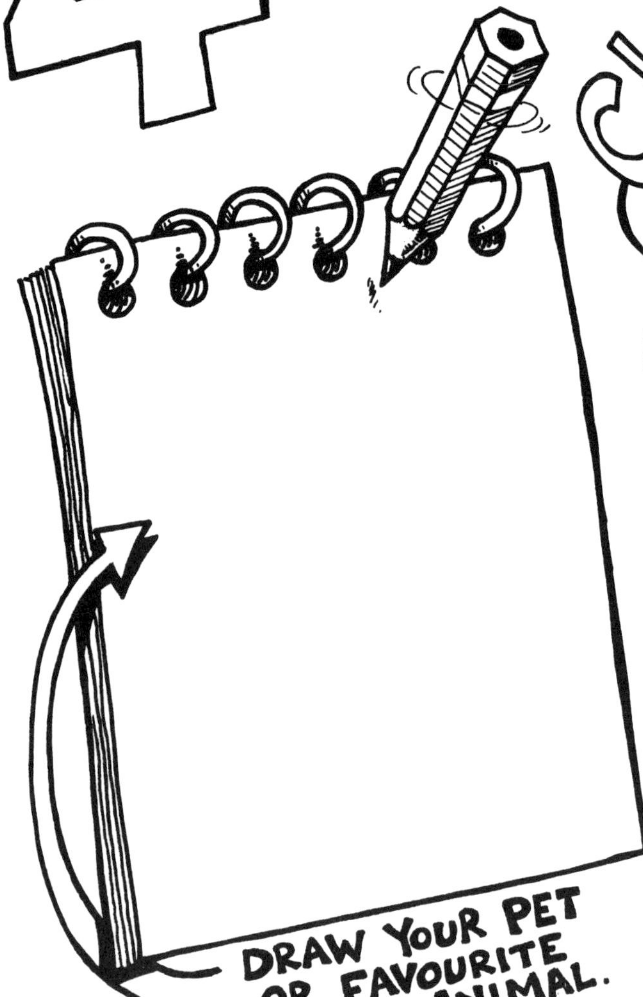

DRAW YOUR PET OR FAVOURITE ANIMAL.

Mrs Noah

What do you think Mrs Noah thought?

O	D	O	G	Q	P	A	F	A
S	O	K	B	L	E	N	R	M
R	E	B	A	C	L	I	O	N
H	I	I	N	D	E	S	G	T
P	L	A	T	Y	P	U	S	I
U	A	E	E	V	H	J	E	G
M	M	F	U	C	A	T	T	E
A	B	S	T	O	N	M	U	R
G	A	K	Q	M	T	S	P	O
J	T	S	P	I	D	E	R	P

Find these 12 animals

Tiger
Frog
Ant
Cat
Lion
Elephant
Platypus
Dog
Doe
Puma
Spider
Lamb

Session 3 Love for . . . friends

Theme

Friendship is part of God's plan for all of us – he wants us to have friends and care about them.

Game

My friend
Invite two friends to the front, one of whom leaves the room while you ask the other the following questions:

- What is your friend's favourite food?
- What is your friend's worst habit?
- Where would your friend love to have a holiday?

Invite the friend back in, and ask him the same questions about himself. Award one point for each answer that is the same as the one the friend gave. Then ask the other friend to leave the room, and ask the same questions of the remaining one, and repeat the process.

Active game

Finding friends
Everyone should be standing in a large room. Then ask them to move around and find a friend who shares the same tastes in the following subjects and stand by them:

pop music	food
pets	games and sport
hobbies	colours
football team	school subjects

Illustration

Have some photographs of when you were young, preferably photos including friends. Talk about your friends, and why you enjoyed spending time with them. Try to describe what it was like to fall out with a friend and how you felt when friendships went wrong.

Bible Input

Use this account of the story of the friendship between David and Jonathan, with the group using the response *They were good friends* every time you say 'good friends'.

Saul was the king. He had been a really good king, but as he got older he started to do and think strange things. He began to think that one of his best soldiers and servants, David, was trying to take over his kingdom.

Jonathan was King Saul's son. He supported and loved his father, but he also loved his best friend, David. Jonathan would do anything for his friend David, they were good friends *(They were good friends).*

David was a hero to the people. When he was still a boy he had bravely stood before a giant. The giant, Goliath, had laughed at this little boy until David, using a sling and a stone, killed him. David grew up into a good soldier and musician, and he would write songs and play a harp to calm King Saul down when he was angry. Then the king's son and David became good friends *(They were good friends).*

King Saul became more and more jealous of David. Each time David would go away for a few days and hide until his friend Jonathan came to tell him it was safe again, and the king had calmed down. They were good friends *(They were good friends).*

Sometimes Jonathan would talk to his father about David, and try to explain that David was a good man and had done lots of things to help King Saul. Jonathan put himself at risk, and his father even threw a spear at him in anger. But still Jonathan wanted to help, because he and David were good friends *(They were good friends).*

In the end David was so afraid that King Saul would kill him that he decided to leave. Jonathan and David met in field near to Saul's palace and talked, cried and hugged. They had been such good friends *(They were good friends),* and now they were having to part. It wasn't many months afterwards that Jonathan was killed in battle and Saul died. Then David was welcomed back to the country as the new king. But he never forgot Jonathan, who was his really good friend *(They were good friends).*

Quiz

Stand the group in the middle of the room and label one wall 'Yes', and the opposite wall 'No'. Then read out these statements, some of which relate to the story about David and Jonathan, and some of which are more general. The children should move to the place they think is right (Yes or No).

1.	Jonathan killed the giant called Goliath.	No
2.	David and Jonathan were brothers.	No
3.	Friends should do all they can to help each other.	Yes
4.	King Saul became jealous of David.	Yes
5.	Jonathan agreed with his father about David.	No
6.	Friends should enjoy being together.	Yes
7.	Jonathan and David were friends from childhood.	No
8.	David was afraid of Jonathan's father.	Yes
9.	Friendships don't usually last long.	No
10.	Jonathan and David escaped from Saul together	No
11.	Jonathan was afraid for David's safety.	Yes
12.	David and Jonathan are a good example of friendship.	Yes

Craft and prayer

Give the group small pieces of card and something to write with. Ask them to make a list of all their friends, and then invite them to sit quietly and look at the list while you say this prayer:

Thank you, God, for friends.
Thank you that you love us so much
that you let us have friends to help us,
to keep us happy
and to be there in bad times.
Thank you for my friends,
and help me to be a good friend for them.
Amen.

Memory chant

Learn this one this time:

God shows love that never ends
by sending us our closest friends.

Songs

Thank you, Lord
I'm special
God loves me
Jesus' love is very wonderful

LOVE 4

3. Love for... Friends.

DAVID and JONATHAN

Number the pictures in order...

○ Jonathan and David were good friends.

○ David had to leave.

○ Saul was the King.

○ As a boy, David killed a giant.

○ Jonathan tried to talk to his father.

THANKS...

Write a message thanking God for your friends...

ALBUM

Draw your best friends here

Chant

God shows love that never ends, by sending us our closest friends.

Session 4 Love for . . . the desperate

Theme

God shows his love for people who do not know what to do or where to go.

Active game

Desperation

Place ten sheets of newspaper or carpet tiles on the floor; ask the children to keep walking around the room while you start counting down from 10. They have to have at least one foot standing on a tile or sheet by the time you have counted down to 0. Then repeat, counting down from 2, then 5, then 7, and so on. Each time by the time you reach 0 the children will be experiencing both excitement and desperation!

Game

Desperate stories

You will need a bell or whistle. Ask for a few volunteers to come out to the front, and explain that they have to continue the story you begin, and when you blow the whistle or ring the bell the story moves on to the next person in the line. Begin with this:

The children were a long way from home, and feeling cold and tired. They were beginning to get a little desperate when . . .

Talk

Most of us will not know what it feels like to be really desperate. We may have felt upset or lonely from time to time, and things may have gone wrong for us. But feeling really desperate is much more serious. People can get desperate if they think that someone they love doesn't love them any more, or if they fear they are going to die. The people of God felt desperate when they were out in the desert after escaping from slavery in Egypt. They had seen one amazing miracle when all the water in a great sea seemed to be held back by God and they were able to walk across the dry sea bed. But, by the time we reach the story, things were beginning to get desperate again. Many were thirsty, others were hungry, and all of them were tired from walking day after day, month after month. We have probably never come close to experiencing such desperation.

Bible input

Exodus 16:1-16
Read this passage from an appropriate version of the Bible or tell it in your own words. Remember to cover these points:

- The people were desperate, but didn't fully trust God.
- They moaned about being hungry, and didn't know where any food could come from.
- Moses prayed, and God told him what to do.
- God spoke to all the people, proving that he loved them.
- God sent quails (small birds) for them to catch.
- God sent manna, like small bits of white bread.
- God loved them by giving them enough food to eat.

Discussion

Talk about how God had already proved he loved the people, but still they moaned.

God showed he loved the desperate people by giving them enough to eat. What desperate people are there that we know about? Make sure that you introduce thinking about the homeless, hungry, lonely, and so on. Do we think that God really loves those people? What can we do to show God's love to them?

Craft

Work together on producing an acrostic of the word 'Desperate'. Write 'Desperate' down the left-hand side of a large piece of paper, and ask for suggestions of what could be put next to each letter, or use these ideas:

D	Don't give up
E	Enjoy what you have
S	Seek help
P	Pray
E	Everything will come good
R	Rely on God's love
A	Always trust
T	Tell others your needs
E	Enjoy what God gives

The group can help to decorate the finished poster by colouring it, drawing relevant pictures, and so on.

Song

Desperate words
Split the group into two or three smaller groups. Ask them each to think of a familiar and popular tune, either a song you sing in the sessions or another one. Then set them the challenge of writing words about the desperate people fed by God to fit the tune they have chosen. This is not an easy activity and they will need a little guidance, but do try to allow time for creativity!

Prayer

Say this prayer after teaching the response 'You show your love'.

Thank you, God, that when people are desperate
You show your love.
Thank you that when desperate people call out to you
You show your love.
Thank you that you really care for the lonely
You show your love.
Thank you that you really care for sad and hurt people
You show your love.
Thank you that you care for those without friends or homes
You show your love.
Thank you, God, that when people are desperate
You show your love.

Memory chant

This is the one for this session:

When we're desperate we should learn
that God is where we need to turn!

Songs

Nobody's a nobody
I will not be afraid
My God shall supply all my needs
God is so good

LOVE 4

4. Love for ... the Desperate.

Chant

Fill in the gaps about God's desperate people.

'The people were ________ but didn't know how to find any ______. Moses ________, and God told him to trust. Then God ______ Small birds and ______ for , the people to _____.

food eat prayed hungry manna sent

Colour in the dotted shapes

Fill in the faces

Session 5 Love for . . . the poor

Theme

God cares for those who others think don't matter, including the poor.

Active game

Leap-frog
Play a simple game of leap-frog. Choose one or two children to be the money-takers, while the others run about the room. When the money-taker tags a child they have to crouch down and wait for another child to leap over them. Let the game continue until the children have used up some of their energy.

Illustration

Continue the game with one money-taker and one child – it won't last long! Explain that for many reasons people become poor, through money-takers of all kinds. The child who was tagged by the money-taker had to wait until someone helped them by jumping over them, but they can't get back into the game if no one helps.

Discussion

Ask the children to discuss, in twos or threes, the reasons why people may become poor. You may need to be sensitive to those children who are not from wealthy backgrounds themselves. Make sure that in the discussion you include:

- It is not always the person's fault if they become poor.
- Poor people need others to help them.
- There are still many poor people in rich countries.
- Being poor doesn't make the person less important.
- God loves poor people as much as he loves anyone else.

Craft

Have and need
You will need:

- enough large (at least 20 cm diameter) circles of card for all the children
- pens
- pencils
- scissors
- wool

Show the children how to mark each side around the edge with small lines to make it look like a large coin. On one side they should write 'Wants' and on the other 'Needs'. Then they should draw and colour things which they consider they need on the 'Needs' side, and on the other side things they like to have but don't really need. You could put a hole in these and thread wool through so that they become a mobile.

You may want to look at some of the coins and discuss them once they are completed, reminding the group that there is a difference between essential things and other comfort and fun items. Make it clear that people who are really poor do not even have the essential things.

Game

Guess the goods

Have a large bag such as a bin bag, and some or all of the items listed below inside it. You will also need an empty bag. Then invite two pairs of children to stand on either side of you, each pair with a sheet of paper and a pencil.

Take out the items from the full bag, show them to the children for about five seconds, and then put them into the empty bag. After all the items have been shown the children have to write down as many of them as they can remember. Please be aware that some of the children may need help writing. The winning pair is the one which remembered most items.

carrot	cuddly toy
pencil	book
potato	CD
hairbrush	scarf
shoe	bar of chocolate
toy car	coins

Bible input

Read this version of the Bible story (1 Kings 17:8-16). Before you begin mention that prophets were God's messengers; they were usually poor, and they moved from town to town staying wherever they could.

Elijah was a prophet. He was walking from one town to another when God spoke to him. God told him to go to a small town near Sidon where a poor widow would feed him, so off he went. When Elijah reached the edge of the town he saw a woman collecting firewood.

Elijah was tired, hungry and thirsty. 'Please could you bring me some water, and perhaps something to eat?' he asked her. The woman looked sad, and told Elijah that she had very little food for herself and her son, but they would share it.

Soon Elijah was sitting talking to the widow and her son. The widow explained that the flour jar was nearly empty, and there was only a drop of oil in the oil jar. 'Don't worry,' said Elijah. 'Make a loaf of bread and there will be enough.' The widow did so, and they all ate what she thought would be their last meal. But next day she went to the flour and oil jars and found that they had plenty in them. It seemed that the more she used, the more was there.

Elijah knew that God was showing his love for the poor widow and her son. God was making the jars full of flour and oil, and God cared about them.

Discussion

Talk about how God showed love for the widow, her son and the prophet Elijah. Ask whether the children think God can do things like that now, and how we can help people who are poor. Remind them that being poor doesn't mean not having 'wants', but not having 'needs' such as food and shelter.

Prayer

Put out the items which were used in the 'Guess the goods' game earlier. Spend some time looking at them, and then end by saying this short prayer:

Thank you, God, for all the things we have.
Thank you for the things we need,
and the things we want.
Thank you that you love those who do not have much.
Amen.

Memory chant

Learn this chant this time:

Whether you need less or more,
God has love for rich and poor.

Songs

Will you follow
Safe in the Father's hands
How does sun shine
Lord you gave me

LOVE 4

5. Love for ... the Poor.

ELIJAH

Link the words to the pictures.

Elijah walked from town to town.

*

He visited Sidon, where he met a poor widow.

*

She made bread for Elijah and her son.

*

She was amazed that there was more flour the next day.

BEING POOR

Circle the words that describe how poor people might feel...

left out

rejected

jealous

lonely

upset

cold

rich

hungry

cheerful

sad

unimportant

Chant

Whether you need less or more,
God has love for rich and poor!

Session 6 Love for . . . enemies

Theme

God gives us an example of how we should love those people who seem to hate us.

Active game

Enemies and friends
The children should walk around talking to each other, with body language and facial expressions which display the mood you shout out. Remind them that fighting or hitting as part of the game is not allowed! Here's a list of moods:

friendly	angry
as an enemy	kind
concerned	hurrying
sad	unkind

Discussion

Ask the children to get into small groups and talk about the sort of people they would describe as enemies. Possibilities could include brothers or sisters, neighbours, other children at school, even parents and teachers! Then bring the group together and try to ask these questions, encouraging a range of children to answer:

- How do you feel about your enemies?
- Do you think you are someone else's enemy?
- Should enemies suffer?

Activity

Give each member of the group a piece of paper and a pencil. Ask them to write down as many words as they can think of which describe how they feel about their enemy, or how they imagine people feel about enemies.

Craft

You will need:

- A5 sheets and one A3 sheet of paper
- pens and crayons

Discuss the words the children wrote down about how they feel towards enemies. Then make a list of some of them, enough for one for each child. Ask each child to choose a word and then write it on an A5 piece of paper, colour it in and cut around it. Meanwhile get an A3 sheet of paper and write on it in large letters 'God loves enemies'. Then stick the children's words on to the A3 sheet and put the poster up in the room where you meet.

Bible input

Read the Bible passage from Acts 16:23-34 or tell it in your own words. You will need to cover the following points, asking after some of them, 'What would you do?' and allowing the children time to discuss and respond:

- Paul and Silas were visiting the town of Philippi to speak about Jesus there.
- Paul and Silas were thrown into prison even though they were doing nothing wrong.
  What would you do?
- They didn't moan about what their enemy, the jailer, did to them.
- Paul and Silas spent their time praising God by singing and praying.
  What would you do?
- The earthquake made their chains fall off – they were free to go.
  What would you do?
- They knew that the jailer would be in big trouble if they escaped.
- They decided to stay, and spoke to the jailer when he arrived.
  What would you do?
- The jailer was amazed that they had stayed, and wanted to know more about their God and his love.
- The jailer and all his family then believed and trusted God.

Quiz

Put up the answers to these questions around the walls of the room. Split the group into two teams, and ask for one volunteer from each to be the 'runner'. After you have asked each question the runners should consult with their teams and then run to the correct answer, the first there gaining a point for their team.

1. What was Paul's friend called?	Silas
2. Who did they want to speak about?	Jesus
3. What was the name of the town?	Philippi
4. What had they done to be thrown into prison?	Nothing
5. What did they do to pass the time?	Praised God
6. What made their chains fall off?	Earthquake
7. What do you think the other prisoners did?	Escaped
8. Who came to find them?	Jailer

Talk

God shows us that it is right to love those who seem to hate us. Jesus told people to keep forgiving time and time again, otherwise the hate can eat us up and make us feel really bad inside. But it is hard to love those who seem to hate us. Paul and Silas showed both their love and God's love for the jailer and his family. They could have left him to suffer, even though he would probably have been executed for letting them go. Instead they put his need before their own, and helped him understand God's love through it.

Prayer

Use the poster you made earlier to help with the prayer, saying one of the words the children drew and stuck on after each phrase, repeating it until you have said all the words. Use the response 'Help me to love everyone'.

Dear God, help me to love the people who ...
Help me to love everyone.

Memory chant

Here's this session's chant:

God shows us what we should do,
how to love our enemies too!

Songs

Make me a channel of your peace
God's love will never end
Live my life by faith
Give me oil in my lamp

LOVE 4

6. Love for… Enemies.

IN PRISON

Silas praised God:

After the earthquake the jailer said:

Paul stopped the jailer from killing himself:

THE END

Finish the story by unravelling the words:

'The [lajrei] was amazed, and he and his [lamyfi] then [veedlieb] and [sturdet] in God' Acts 16:34

Enemies

Make a list of people who upset you, and try to love them!

Chant

God shows us what we should do, how to love our enemies too!

Session 7 Love for . . . families

Theme

God loves families; they are part of his plan for people.

Game

Happy families

Buy some inexpensive packs of cards for the game 'Happy families' and play it in small groups. Many of the children may never have played it before, so you may need to organise a demonstration game before they start.

Active game

Family groups

You will need a tape player and tape. Ask all the children to stand in the middle of the room. When the music stops they should get into imaginary family groups, which you describe from the list below, and stand as still as possible. The children should kneel, and older ones stand, posing as the members of the family they represent. Some boys may have to play the role of girls, and vice versa!

- Father, mother, one boy, one girl
- Grandmother, mother, two boys
- Father, one girl and two boys
- Both grandparents, three children
- Father and mother, one child
- Mother, two girls and two boys

Discussion

Talk about how families come in different shapes and sizes. All of us are in one type of family or another, and many of us are in families that have changed with new arrivals or people leaving the family. Explain that being in a family is the best way to be, and God designed families for us to live in. He wants us to feel happy, content and settled in our families. Remember as you discuss this that some of the group may be from complex family backgrounds.

Craft

My family

You will need:

- paper
- crayons
- scissors
- thread

Each of the children should draw a circle as large as possible on the paper, and then draw a spiral pattern moving from the outside to the centre. Near the centre of the circle they should draw their own face, followed by others in their family. Their extended family (grandparents, cousins, etc.) should be drawn further towards the edge. Once the faces are finished and coloured in, the spiral can carefully be cut out, so that it looks a little like a curled up snake! Then put a hole in one end, put some thread through, and hang it as a mobile.

Talk

God loves families and wants them to stick together, but even so things go wrong. People find that they do not love each other any more, or they get jealous of each other. Even the first brothers in the world, Cain and Abel, got angry with each other and it ended in death! (See an outline on this story in the companion book, *Ten Commandments.)*

But God cares about families, and he wants them to be happy.

Bible input

Read this version of the story of Abraham, Isaac and Sarah (Genesis 21:1-8, 22:1-19). If possible, get children to act out the five characters: Sarah, Isaac, Abraham and two servants.

Abraham and Sarah were very happy. God had been with them all their lives, and now they had a child, a son called Isaac. They hadn't expected to have a son because they were very old, but God had promised that it would happen, and God keeps his promises!

Isaac was a lively boy, and his parents loved him very much. They were proud of the way he was learning to fish, to hunt, and the way he showed his love for them. As far as Abraham and Sarah were concerned, everything was perfect.

One day God spoke to Abraham as he often did. God told Abraham to take his only son, Isaac, up the mountain and build an altar (a sort of barbecue) made out of stones. Then God told Abraham that he had to kill Isaac and put him on the altar. Abraham couldn't believe it, and it made him sad and angry. He didn't understand why God would want him to give up his own child. But Abraham had learned over his many years that it is always best to obey God, so he got ready to go.

Sarah watched as Abraham, Isaac and the servants set off into the distance. She shook her head – why were they going off to the mountain? She just didn't understand. She waved as they went out of sight.

Isaac asked his father where they were going. Abraham explained that they were going up the mountain to build an altar for God. Isaac couldn't understand why they didn't have an animal with them to put on the altar. As they got near the place Abraham sent the servants away and he and Isaac built the altar. Then the time Abraham had been dreading came near, and he was about to kill Isaac when God said, 'Stop! I was testing whether you loved me as much as I love you and your family. Don't harm Isaac; find an animal and put that on the altar instead.' Abraham was very relieved, and so was Isaac! God went on to promise Abraham that he would be the founder of a large family, and many thousands of people would look back on Abraham as their father, grandfather, great grandfather, and so on.

Talk

Explain that God loves families, and even though he tested Abraham, he didn't really want Isaac or any of Abraham's family to suffer harm. God loves our families too, even if they are sometimes unhappy.

Prayer

Say this prayer, repeating it and asking the children to concentrate on it really hard each time:

Dear God, we thank you for our families.
Thank you for those who look after us
and show their love through what they do.
Help us when our families fight,
or when things are not happy at home.
Help us to love our families as much as you do.
Amen.

Memory chant

The memory chant for this session is:

Help me know and help me see
that God loves every family!

Songs

As for me and my house
God's family
God is here
God is good, God is great

LOVE 4

7. Love for... Families.

ABRAHAM

ISAAC

SARAH

Chant

Help me know and
help me see,
that God
loves
every family
!

GOOD + BAD THINGS ABOUT FAMILIES

✓ the good things, X the bad things

happiness
TV
busy bathroom
computer use
jealousy
arguments
anger
favourites
no money
love
mealtimes

FAMILY PRAYER

Finish this

Father God,
thank you
for my family.
Thank you for

____

____

____

____

__________. Amen.

My Family

DRAW A FAMILY 'PHOTO' HERE

Session 8 Love for . . . the sad

Theme

God loves people who are upset or have deep problems. God is always willing to help.

Craft

You will need:
- paper
- pens and crayons
- scissors
- thin canes or sticks
- glue

The children should draw and colour in a very happy face on one sheet of paper, and a very miserable one on another. Then the faces should be stuck back to back, with the stick down the middle so they can be held like a lollipop. These will be used in the 'Happy and sad' game which follows.

Active game

Happy and sad

Split the group into pairs, and have all the pairs sitting in the middle of the room. Read out each of the statements below (some of which need to be adapted to local circumstances). The pairs should discuss whether the statement is a happy or sad one, and stand showing the appropriate faces once they have decided. To add a competitive edge those who are in the minority should sit out for the rest of the game!

- It rains all day on a Saturday.
- (Local football team) win.
- (Local football team) lose.
- School is unexpectedly closed.
- You lose your pocket money.
- It is your turn to wash up at home.
- Your brother or sister gets injured in a game.
- The TV blows up just before *Top of the Pops*.
- Steps (or another pop group) come to visit this group.
- Your mother becomes ill.
- You miss out on a school trip to (local boring beauty spot).
- You miss out on a school trip to Disneyland.
- You get a love letter at school.
- Fish and chips is served up for tea.

Discussion

Talk about some of the things that make the children sad, including some of those from the list. Ask the children who feel able to talk about times they have been sad and how they coped with it. Cover these questions:

- What makes you really sad inside?
- How do you cope when you are feeling sad?
- What makes you happy again?
- What things do you think make your parent(s) sad?
- What do you think makes God sad?

Bible input

Read out the story (Mark 5:21-24, 35-43) from a suitable version of the Bible. You could ask some of the children to act out the key parts (Jairus, Jesus, servant, daughter) and the others play the part of the crowds. Afterwards make sure that you cover the following points:

- Jairus was an important man, but he knew he needed Jesus to help.
- Jesus was busy and crowded, and he didn't have to do what Jairus wanted.
- Jairus was very sad about the illness of his daughter.
- Jesus cared about Jairus' sadness and wanted to help.
- Jesus knew that Jairus and all the other people didn't need to be sad.

Talk

Jesus cared for Jairus and many other people in the crowd too. Jairus felt sad because his daughter was ill, but there are many reasons why people feel sad. Sometimes we feel sad about things we have done that have caused us pain or got us into trouble. Whatever the reason for our sadness, God offers to help us and make us feel better. He doesn't always make things change instantly, but he does know how we feel and he always loves us.

Prayer

Play some quiet music, asking the children to sit quietly with their eyes closed and listen. Quietly and slowly mention some of the reasons why people become sad which the children brought up and discussed earlier. Allow a few moments more for the children to listen to the music before turning it off and asking them to open their eyes.

Memory chant

This is the next one to be learned:

God loves us when things are bad,
God loves all who feel sad!

Songs

God knows me (especially verse 2)
God has got a plan
When I am hurt
I believe in Jesus

LOVE 4

8. Love for ... the Sad.

JAIRUS JESUS

JESUS VISITED A VILLAGE WHERE A LARGE CROWD WAS WAITING...

... JAIRUS BEGGED JESUS TO HELP HIS DAUGHTER...

... JAIRUS' DAUGHTER WAS ALIVE, AND EVERYONE WAS AMAZED.

FILL IN THE PICTURES...

✓ and ✗

Write down GOOD ✓ and BAD ✗ things that happen to you or others.

✓	✗

Chant

God loves us when things are bad,
God loves all who feel sad!

Session 9 Love for . . . the unwanted

Theme

God loves everyone, even those who are unwanted by others.

Active game

Bring out . . .

Split the children into three or four groups sitting at equal distances from you as you stand in the middle of the room. Then name each of the items in turn from the list below. The first (or only) group to bring the item to you gains a point.

watch	shoe
a dark hair	comb
handkerchief	bag
drawing pin	pen
sock	book
piece of paper	cup
shirt	coin
plant	Bible
jumper	ring

Game

Rubbish bin

Place in the centre of the room a large pile of pieces of paper with the words given below written on them. Ask for two volunteers to come forward and give each a bin bag to take back to their corner. Allow them one minute to run from the bag to the pile, pick up a maximum of three pieces of paper at a time, and run back to put them in their bin bags. Encourage the other children to cheer them on, and after one minute count up the totals in each bag. The winner will be the one with the most. If there is time you could repeat the game with other children.

sick	old
poor	lonely
special needs	young
difficult	different

Discussion

Look at the pieces of paper used in the last game, and discuss each one in turn. All of these types of people may feel unwanted because others don't know what they can do, or how to talk to them. Remind the children that there may be people in the community who are teased or bullied because of what they are like or what they can't do. This is the wrong way to be.

Try to bring out:

- Unwanted people need someone to love them.
- We should never make anyone feel unwanted.
- God loves everyone, whatever they are like.
- We should love everyone as God does.

Bible input

Read this version of the story of Jesus healing a boy, which is based on Luke 9:37-43.

There was a boy who lived in one of the *villages* Jesus often visited. He was a normal boy apart from when he had *fits.* From time to time he would *fall* over, cry out, and fight anyone who tried to calm him. His *father* was very worried about him but didn't know what to do. On a few occasions the boy had fallen into a *fire* and burned himself, while another time he had fallen into a pond and nearly *drowned.* Some people said that there was *evil* inside the boy, and nobody really wanted anything to do with him.

When Jesus visited the *village* the boy's father stopped him and explained about his son. He told Jesus that his son was *unwanted* by everyone because of the fits he kept having, and that he didn't know what to do about it. Jesus told him not to *worry* and asked to see the boy. The boy was just *starting* to have another fit when Jesus prayed for him and the *fit* stopped. The people were amazed, the father was grateful, and everyone realised that Jesus had God's *love* and power.

Active game

Sit all the children on the floor and repeat the reading of the Bible story above, missing out the italicised words. Ask the children to think of the word that is missing and stand up when they have done so. Choose one of the standing children to fill in the gap. Repeat for the next missing word, and so on.

Talk

Hold one of the bin bags while you talk.

There are many people whom the world doesn't seem to want. We are all guilty of teasing others or leaving them out of a game. We all think badly of people who walk differently or who can't do the things we can do. This is not the way God wants it to be. He loves everyone, even the people we may think should be thrown into the bin and whom we don't want anything to do with. God's love is for everyone, even the unwanted. Ours should be too.

Prayer

Put the pieces of paper with unwanted people around the walls of the room. Ask the children to move from one to the other, saying private prayers to God for these people who may feel unwanted. End by asking the children to stand still and listen to you as you say this prayer:

Thank you, God, that you love everyone.
We are sorry for the times
we have made other people feel unwanted.
Help us to show your love for all people too.
Amen.

Memory chant

This is the one this time:

God's great love goes on and on
for every poor, unwanted one!

Songs

I'm special
Will you follow
Don't be an actor
I once was frightened
I will not be afraid

LOVE 4

9. Love for ... the Unwanted.

Chant

God's great love goes on and on,
For every poor, unwanted one.

S	A	D	Q	X	D	F	R
P	J	A	W	S	I	C	K
S	M	I	H	V	F	E	S
E	L	M	U	D	F	L	N
P	O	O	R	J	E	K	E
O	N	L	T	A	R	G	E
S	E	D	U	Y	E	T	D
N	L	Y	O	U	N	G	Y
H	Y	B	C	I	T	Z	B
A	S	P	E	C	I	A	L

UNWANTED PEOPLE

FIND THESE 10 WORDS:

SAD DIFFERENT
NEEDY SICK
LONELY OLD
POOR YOUNG
HURT SPECIAL

HEALED!

Fill in what the crowd thought when the boy was healed...

Write a prayer thanking God that he loves all people:

Session 10 Love for . . . us

Theme

God's love is for everyone else and for us too. He wants us to really know what it is to be loved by him.

Bible input 1

Tell this familiar story, with children acting it out to create a nativity scene.

Mary and Joseph arrived in Bethlehem, tired and fed up. They needed somewhere to sleep but because the town was full of visitors they had to make do with a cold, damp stable. It was there that Mary, who was expecting a special baby, gave birth to a boy she called Jesus.

On the hillsides around the town shepherds were watching their sheep and protecting them from attack. Some shepherds were shocked to see the sky open up and a crowd of angels singing. The angels told the shepherds that a new king had been born and was in a stable in the town. The shepherds dashed off to see what all the fuss was about.

Three very wise men had been travelling for months following a star that shone in the sky. They knew from old books that the star would lead them to a new king. Eventually they arrived in Bethlehem, and went to visit the baby Jesus.

Active game

Find a person
The children should move around the room and try to find and stand by a person you describe. For most of these they will need to talk to each other to discover whether they fit your description.

- Find a person who has two brothers.
- Find a person who has a new baby at home.
- Find a person who knows all about stars.
- Find a person who had chips for tea yesterday.
- Find a person who likes watching cartoons.
- Find a person who sees grandparents every week.
- Find a person who likes maths at school.
- Find a person who has a tidy bedroom.
- Find a person who has been to the USA.
- Find a person who is a good singer.

Illustration

Have another leader come into the room looking worried and distracted, with their glasses propped up in their hair or on a cord around their neck. They are obviously looking for something, and won't be distracted from it. Try to stop him/her, and keep asking what it is that he/she is searching for. In the end the leader should stop and say that they are looking for their glasses, and they have no idea where they are! By now the children should be able to point out where the specs are!

Talk

That leader was looking for his/her glasses, but they were there all the time. The shepherds left their sheep to look for the new king, Jesus. The wise men travelled for many months in order to find and see Jesus. Jesus came to earth so that people didn't have to search for God. He lived as an ordinary child and grew up into a very special man to show that God's love is everywhere, and for everyone . . . including us. We don't have to go on long journeys or searches to find God – like the leader's specs, he is with us all the time.

Craft

God loves . . .

You will need:

- books made up of five sheets of A5 paper stapled in the middle
- pencils and crayons

The books should be worked on with the hinge/staples at the top, and on each page the children can draw and colour the words and pictures for each of the themes in this series:

- God loves the world
- God loves animals
- God loves friends
- God loves the desperate
- God loves the poor
- God loves enemies
- God loves family
- God loves the sad
- God loves the unwanted
- God loves me!

Bible input 2

Read an account of the death of Jesus or describe it in your own words. Make sure you cover these key points:

- Jesus was sentenced to death although he had done nothing wrong.
- He carried his own cross up the hill towards where he would die.
- He was put on the cross, and alongside were two thieves.
- As Jesus was dying he called out to his Father God.

- As he died the sky went dark.
- To make sure he was dead a soldier stabbed him.
- His dead body was taken down and put in a tomb.

Discussion

Talk about why Jesus died. Try to get the children to understand that he died for all of us, so that we could know the love of God for ourselves. God loves us, and showed that love through sending his Son Jesus to live as a man as well as being part of God. But Jesus' death wasn't the end, and he came alive again and lives now. We can know the love of God by believing in him, by trusting him, and by really letting him help us throughout our lives.

Prayer

Copy this prayer on to a large sheet of paper or an OHP sheet so all the children can read it together. Allow them a little time to read it through before you all say it:

The times when I am good and helpful
thank you, God, that you love me.
The times when I am difficult and moody
thank you, God, that you love me.
The times when I am feeling great
and everything is going well
thank you, God, that you love me.
The times when I feel foul and everything is going wrong
thank you, God, that you love me.
At all times, in all places, for all my life
thank you, God, that you love me.
Amen.

Memory chant

This is the last one of the series to learn:

Thank you, God, that now we see
you love us, and you love me!

Songs

God's love will never end
Father God, I wonder
The Lord loves me
When I think about the cross
For God so loved the world

LOVE 4

10. Love for ... Us.

JESUS - Beginning and End

Visit
wise
special
born

Jesus was _____ in a stable. Shepherds went to ____ him and three ____ men knew that the baby Jesus was _______.

Forgiven
hung
everyone
done

Jesus was _____ on a cross although he had _____ nothing wrong. He was willing to die for _____ so that we can be _______.

GOD LOVES ME!

Chant

Thank you God,
that now we see,
you love us,
and you love me!

Circle those that God loves...

GOD LOVES

family
us
everyone
me
the unwanted
enemies
the poor
the desperate
animals
friends
the world
sad people